Revolutionary Constructive Resistance
Benin 1989 in context and perspective

Revolutionary Constructive Resistance -
Benin 1989 in context and perspective

by Jørgen Johansen and Stellan Vinthagen

First published 2019 by
Irene Publishing

Sparsnäs 1010
66891 Ed

Sweden

irene.publishing@gmail.com

ISBN 978-91-88061-36-2

Layout: J. Johansen

Cover: Symbol for the 30th anniversary of the events.

Creative Common License

Revolutionary Constructive Resistance - Benin 1989 in context and perspective

Jørgen Johansen and Stellan Vinthagen

Contents

Waves of Peaceful Revolutions	5
Benin prior to the Revolution	10
Complex and Manifold Causes	12
Economy in Bad Shape	13
The role of the International Context	15
Religious Division Lines	16
Human Rights	17
Conférence Nationale des Forces Vives	17
Civil Society in Benin	23
Information and Communication	31
Reasons for the Protest, Sources of Inspiration and Results	32
Seven Cases of "Conférences Nationales"	37
Conclusions	45
References	49

Waves of peaceful revolutions[1]

During the last forty years political revolutions have taken place on four continents without major use of violence from those who have demanded change. From Poland 1980-89 all the way to Algeria 2019, one can see seven "waves" where massive civil society[2] mobilization has made demands from, or managed to overturn or reform, the ruling regime. These waves are not clearly delineated and do not follow a strict chronological order, but can still be grouped according to their similarities.

In the first wave we have Poland, Bolivia 1982, Uruguay 1984 and the Philippines 1986. This wave had one important common denominator: the Catholic Church played a significant role in Eastern Europe (Luxmoore and Babiuch, 1999) and the other Catholic states through Liberation Theology (Gutiérrez, 1973, Dunkerley, 1984, Malloy and Gamarra, 1988).

The next wave was Eastern Europe from 1989, concerning and the parts of the Soviet Union that liberated themselves and became independent states in a peaceful manner (Sixsmith, 1991, Legters, 1992, Wheaton and Kavan, 1992, Opp et al., 1995, Cirtautas, 1997, Grix, 2000, Petersen, 2001, Stjernø, 2005, Sarotte, 2009, Sebestyen, 2010, Bunce and Wolchik, 2011).

After this, there came a wave consisting mainly of former French colonies in Africa, south of the Sahara. It is this group, especially the case of Benin, that this article will be concerned with (Decalo, 1997, Seely, 2005, Gisselquist, 2008, Seely, 2009). Benin was followed by six other states: Congo February 1990, Gabon March 1990, Zaïre

---

1. We are extremely grateful to Shibani Pandya and Craig S Brown for skillful and efficient language editing and editorial help with this text. This text would not have been possible without generous support from ICNC.
2.- The concept of "civil society" is discussed and defined below.

February 1991, Togo July/August 191, Niger July 1992, and Chad January 1993 (Nwajiaku, 1994, p. 429).

The next wave started with Serbia 2000 and continued with Georgia 2003, Ukraine 2004 and has thus far reached Kyrgyzstan and Lebanon 2005. These are called the colored revolutions (Peczak and Krajewska-Wieczorek, 1991, Kuzio and Wilson, 1994, Zajovic and Aleksov, 1997, Kandiâc and Fond za humanitarno pravo., 2001, Karumize and Wertsch, 2005, Kuzio, 2005, Paulson, 2005, Wilson, 2005, Åslund and McFaul, 2006, Collin, 2007, Knudsen and Kerr, 2012).

From 2009 onwards, we have seen a number of popular riots in countries with collapsing economies. The "Kitchenware Revolution"[3] in Iceland was first (Reuters, 2009, Waterfield, 2009), followed by the "Penguin Revolution" in Latvia (Forssman, 2009, Huffington Post, 2009), and protests in Hungary (Kulish, 2009) and the Czech Republic (BBC, 2012). In January 2013 the Bulgarian government, led by Boiko Borisov, resigned (Reuters, 2013). A massive demonstration by the victims of a speculative and mismanaged economy forced the government to step down.

In 2011 the so-called "Arab Spring"[4] began and we have, most likely, not seen the end of that wave yet (Gardner, 2011, Korany and El-Mahdi, 2012, Noueihed and Warren, 2012).

In 2018-19 we saw several new uprisings in North Africa with Suadan and Algeria as the two most prominent examples. Algeria's President Bouteflika was forced to resign in April 2019, while in the same month Omar al-Bashir had to resign as president in Sudan. In

---

3. "Busahaldabyltingin" in Icelandic
4. The label "Arab Spring" is misleading in several ways. The uprisings was much more complex than just "arabs" acting during the spring season. Several groups had been protsting for many years prior to events got headlines in western media.

both cases massive protests were a key factor in the changes and the experiences from the latest wave in the MENA region was very much present. Much efforts has been undertaken to reduse the risks of military takeovers, and the demands for civilian participation in the new regimes were loud and prominent. Whether they will succeed is still to be seen.

All these examples have been categorized in a variety of ways. The media has often used expressions such as "peaceful revolutions" or given them names after symbols (Orange in Ukraine (Krushnelnycky, 2006), Rose in Georgia (Karumize and Wertsch, 2005), Cedar in Lebanon (Knudsen and Kerr, 2012) and so forth. Many academic texts have discussed whether they should be called 'peaceful', 'nonviolent', 'unarmed' or whether they should be called revolutions at all.[5]

Cohan (1975) lists six characteristics of a typical revolution:

I. Alteration of the basic values and myths of a society
II. Alteration of the social structure
III. Alteration of social institutions
IV. Changes in the structure of leadership, in terms of either the personnel of the elite or its class composition
V. Non-legal or illegal transfer of power
VI. Presence or dominance of violence in the actions leading a regime to collapse

For point VI it is probably accurate to assume that Cohan means the violence is used by those seeking change. But we have seen that state actors such as police, military, and security forces have used violence even when the opposition abstains from violence. Some of these cases,

---

5. The traditional Marxist connection between revolution and war as a means have led some to argue that violent means are a necessary ingredient of a "proper" revolution. A deep analysis of this connection is made in Peralta's (1990) book. Godwin is discusses the definitions of revolution in his article "Toward a New Sociology of Revolutions" (1994)

like Iran 1979 (Abrahamian, 1982, Hooglund, 1982, Hiller, 1983, Arjomand, 1988, Foran, 1994, Ganji, 2002, Ritter, 2013) have been very bloody, but most of the violence was from one side. In this text we use the term Nonviolent Revolution for cases of what Skocpol calls Political Revolutions (Skocpol, 1979), but add that the opposition shall not use organized armed violence as part of their strategy. In the case of Benin there was not much use of violence by any actor.

Cohan describes revolution as:

> *that process by which a radical alternation of a particular society occurs over a given tome span. Such alternation would include (a) a change in the class composition of the elites, (b) the elimination of previous political institutions and their replacement by other (or by none), or an alternation of the functions of these institutions, and (c) changes in the social structure which would be reflected in the class arrangements and/or the redistribution of resources and income (Cohan, 1975, p. 31).*

This definition excludes cases like Benin. The use of national conferences as a main ingredient in the transition does not necessarily include a change in the class composition of the elite. Neither does it demand elimination of previous political institutions; at least not all of them.

We will not dedicate much space to a debate about terminology. However, in the context that we are discussing the present issue, it is important to see that these events have succeeded in strongly influencing the power of the old regime. This has been done outside the accepted constitutional processes and civil society actors have been central driving forces. The strategies used have not included the use of, or threat, organized armed violence. These peaceful strategies have not necessarily had a pacifistic value system as their basis but neither have they included the use of violence. They instead involved pragmatic evaluations of what possibilities one has had for winning the struggle. It is necessarily so that many contextual factors impact the causes, realization, and outcome of revolutions such as these. The contexts have varied considerably and it is difficult to identify any common factor among all cases.

The fact that many of these peaceful revolutions have taken place in conjunction with elections, where the opposition has made allegations that the rulers have been cheating, is an example of one such contextual factor that we can identify in many, but not all, cases. The same with the media situation; access to means of mass communication has proven to be important in several revolutions. A third example is the existence of support from external actors (Johansen, 2009, Johansen, 2010). In this vein, it has been decisive whether the opposition has been able to create broad alliances. Without a united opposition the chances for victory seem very slim. However, the strength of standing together seldom lasts. What we have seen in several peaceful revolutions is that the unity of the opposition seems to break up as soon as the old regime steps down. The developments in Egypt after the fall of Mubarak are just one more example of the difficulties former opposition groups face when running the country (Korany and El-Mahdi, 2012). Benin had, to some degree, a different development than most other revolutions until 1989-90. The element of cooperation between the opposition and the old regime is unique. When it comes to stability, sustainable democracy and improvement they seem to have succeeded better than most other revolutions.

Analyzing and understanding the contexts is crucial. Economic, cultural, religious and historical facts are determining factors in the possibilities and consequences of political and social uprisings. Skocpol posited that "revolutions cannot be explained without systematic reference to international structures and world-historical developments" (Skocpol, 1979). It is easy to agree.

In this article, we will study the case of transitions in Benin 1989-91 and specifically analyze the roles of: the historical context; the present context; the use on active nonviolence; external actors; sources of inspiration, and the relations between the new leadership and the old regime.

Benin prior to the Revolution

There exists very little English literature on the third and fifth of these waves of regime changes. As always there are exceptions, and *Political Reform in Francophone Africa* (Clark and Gardinier, 1997) is a brilliant example. Another is *The Legacies of Transition Governments in Africa* by Seely (Seely, 2009) and her PhD thesis (Seely, 2001). But neither of these focuses specifically on the use of civil resistance in the transition.

Benin was the state where changes first became apparent and the demands for higher transparency, more political alternatives and the first national congress took place. Benin is a small and very poor country; in 1989 it had approximately 5 million inhabitants and a mean life expectancy of 49 years. By 2010 life expectancy had improved to 56 years and the population had grown to more than 9.5 million (UNICEF, 2013). The 2011 maternal mortality rate per 100,000 births for Benin was 410, compared to 468.9 in 2008 and 587.6 in 1990 (Unites Nations Population Fund, 2011). The education system was in a bad state and over 50% of the population was illiterate (UNICEF, 2013). The national population census in 2002 recorded

59 different ethnic groups in Benin (Heldmann, 2013). French is the official language and a large number of tribal languages is spoken throughout the country.

Benin has a long history[6], but in this context it is relevant to briefly mention that France took control of the territory in 1892 and annexed it within French West Africa. It received greater autonomy in 1958 under the name of the Dahomey Republic and became fully independent on 1 August 1960, after negotiations with France (Kneib, 2006). Subsequently, twelve years of violent conflict caused by ethnic and social dynamics. Military coups succeeded each other and Sourou Apithy, Hubert Maga and Justin Ahomadegbé, each representing different parts of the country, all vied for power. Early in the seventies they agreed on the creation of a presidential council where each had a seat (Collins and Burns, 2007, p. 360). In 1972, Mathie Kérékou led a successful military coup and removed the council. He soon established a Marxist rule with himself as president and leader of the Revolutionary Military Council. Banks and the petroleum industry

Photograph of Mathieu Kérékou taken in Cotonou (Benin) during a state visit of Brazil's Luiz Inácio Lula da Silva. By Ricardo Stuckert ABr - Agência Brasil, CC BY 3.0 br. Kérékou died 2015 at the age of 82.

---

6. The Kingdom of Benin existed from the 13th century and is one of the historical states of West Africa. The state that today goes under the name of Benin is not identical with the historical kingdom.

were nationalized and the country was renamed Benin (Decalo, 1997, p. 44-51). In 1980, Kérékou converted to Islam and called himself Ahmed for a time. In 1982 Benin became a member of the organisation of the Islamic Conference (OIC). Later, he let himself be baptized as a "born again Christian" (IRIN, 2005). At this time he earned the nickname "The Chameleon" due to his constant changes of political and religious identity (Claffey, 2007). This confusing politics can be explained by, among other things, the intent of creating national unity and reducing ethnic and religious tensions. The country consists of 27.1% Catholics, 24.4% Muslims, 18% other Christian factions, 17.3% Vodou[7], 6% traditional animistic religions and 6.5% claiming to have no religious faith (U.S. State Department, 2007). As a Marxist, Kérékou tried to include the left wing in national politics, and with his membership of the OIC he sought support from the Muslim population. He remained president until the peaceful change in 1991. The fact that he was elected again in 1996-2006 is interesting, but not central to the theme of this article.

Complex and Manifold Causes

The opening of the political space in Africa was the result of a very complex interplay between external and internal actors. The end of the Cold War affected Benin, just like other Marxist regimes all over the world. President Kérékou had to struggle with several problems within the country. The army was divided and many feared that Benin would once again be the country with the most military coups in African history. During the eighties the economy was in ruins, and France had already declared that they would no longer save Benin from economic chaos. Economic support form France had been decisive for Kérékou, since he never managed to gain any significant sums of money from his Arabic and Eastern European allies.

In the following we will, in more detail, describe the historical background to the transition that took place in 1989-91.

---

7. A traditional monotheistic religion mainly existing in West Africa.

Economy in Bad Shape

At the beginning of the eighties the country received support from some international lenders and a few other countries. But with a national debt of 677 million dollars in 1985 and a total export of 148 million dollars in the same year, it was obvious that the crisis would soon be absolute. The International Development Association (IDA), Switzerland, West Germany and USSR promised new loans and debt restructuring. However, this did not matter much for the ordinary student or worker. Some promises were never kept. The ones that were did not have any positive impact on those at the base of the societal pyramid.

Ordinary people reacted to the mismanagement, widespread corruption, and moral decay. Benin had a relatively well-developed civil society; especially compared to other African states. There were academic organizations, workplace unions, organized farmers, women and a number of religious organizations. Just as in East Germany, many went into exile. Several people, especially from the higher educated middle class, fled to France. Many left for better education and/or better jobs; others moved because they were so fed up with the double standards and empty promises of the regime. The number of people who left the country exploded so quickly that authorities took action to reduce the number of emigrants. Everyone who left Benin without permission from the state had their property confiscated. Among those who stayed, widespread smuggling of goods from neighboring countries, especially Nigeria, grew. Systems of organized bribes were developed in order for people to pass the borders "unseen". Customs officials, transporters and police officers saw a chance to top up their low salaries. This parallel economy was absolutely necessary for the total economic situation in the country. Many worked with and got their livelihood from the commerce of smuggled goods.

Workers were very disappointed with their "Marxist" government. Salaries had not been raised significantly since 1982 and, due to inflation, purchasing power was reduced significantly. Negotiations with the International Monetary Fund (IMF) broke down in 1984. Kérékou refused to go through with the privatization and deregulation that the IMF demanded (Nugent, 2004, p. 387). This was an especially hard stroke against the country's education system. From the beginning of 1987 students no longer received student grants. They organized a full day strike at Benin University on March 18. According to a communiqué from Party de la Révolution Populaire du Benin (PRPB) broadcast on radio in Cotonou, a small group of "Anarchist students" had created unrest. The party promised that all disturbers would be taken care of and, if necessary, the university would be closed. They also cited the president who said that there should be "no pity" for those who were behind the revolt. (Keesing`s Record of World News 1987, p. 35367) State employees had several of their benefits revoked, and in 1988 the state was no longer able to pay salaries every month. The state was forced to acknowledge this and the union fired its top leader. Shortly afterwards he got the job back by decree of the president. However, the union was not able to keep strict control in the long run. Members organized themselves according to ethnic and ideological lines. In October 1989 the members finally won the struggle, demanding that the union should no longer be formally connected with the dominant state party.

In 1989 Benin's banking system collapsed. This was not solely a result of economic mismanagement. Many employees with high positions in the state banks had embezzled and transferred large amounts of money to foreign bank accounts. When the banks were out of notes, Kérékou's last days of authoritarian rule were over. This acute liquidity crisis resulted in many spontaneous demonstrations and riots in the cities. The regime had difficulty controlling the divided army. The situation that now arose was unprecedented for many of the oppositional groups. They put their conflicts aside and formed a new unified front against president Kérékou and his regime. Such a coalition has shown itself to be decisive in other successful peaceful revolutions.

The role of the International Context

The year was now 1989, and France and most of the present or earlier colonies celebrated the 200-year jubilee of the French Revolution. Seminars, conferences, parades and meetings took place concerning revolutionary history and the 1789 revolution. The events in Benin were similar to those that occurred in France 200 years earlier. The most obvious similarity being the idea of a national congress where the opposition gathered to overthrow the dictatorship and lead the country out of its crisis. Other similarities are that much of the discontent was based on the difficult economic situation, and that strong inspiration came from new ideas. In 1789 it was the enlightenment thoughts of democracy, while 1989 took important inspiration from Eastern Europe and China. In the same way as the different classes were involved in France, many different groups within Benin's society were engaged, not only the Marxist groups.[8] In April and May the people of Benin saw television reports on workers and students in Beijing (Mu et al., 1989, Salisbury, 1989, Yu and Harrison, 1990), who placed revolutionary demands on their regime. Many parts of civil society were in a revolutionary euphoria (Decalo, 1997, p. 53). There were also lively debates about new ideas from Moscow, where Gorbachev had introduced increased openness with perestroika[9] and glasnost[10]

The Storming of the Bastille in the French Revolution

---

8. We wish to thank Majken Jul Sørensen for pointing out the many parallels between these two revolutions. One should make a comparative study of the French Revolution and Benin 200 years later.
9. *Perestrojka* means "restructuring" or "change" and was a name for the new economic politics with less central governance.
10. *Glasnost* means "openness" and was used as a name for the new politics

(Beissinger, 2002). All these were important factors in the events that were to take place.

Religious division lines[11]

The role of religion in the revolutionary process cannot be seen as very important.

According to the 2002 census, 27.1% of the population wass Roman Catholic, 24.4% Muslim, 17.3% Vodou, 5% Celestial Christian, 3.2% Methodist, 7.5% other Christian, 6% other traditional local religious groups, 1.9% other religious groups, and 6.5% claimed no religious affiliation.

Many individuals who nominally identify themselves as Christian or Muslim also practice traditional local religious beliefs. Among the most commonly practiced is the animist Vodou system of belief, also known as voodoo, which originated in this area of Africa.

More than half of all Christians are Catholic. Other religious groups, both Christian and non-Christian, include Baptists, Methodists, Assemblies of God, Pentecostals, Seventh-day Adventists, the Church of Jesus Christ of Latter-day Saints (Mormons), Jehovah's Witnesses, Celestial Christians, Rosicrucians, the Unification Church, Eckankar and Baha'is. Nearly all Muslims adhere to the Sunni branch of Islam. The few Shi'a Muslims are primarily Middle Eastern expatriates.

There are Christians, Muslims and adherents of traditional local religious groups throughout the country. However, most adherents of the traditional Yoruba religious group are in the south, while other local religious beliefs are followed in the north. Muslims are

---

of Gorbachev, with more transparency in public authorities and increased freedom of expression.

11. This chapter is mainly based on International Religious Freedom Report 2007 from the Bureau of Democracy, Human Rights and Labor. http://www.state.gov/j/drl/rls/irf/2007/90082.htm Accessed 2014-09-01

represented most heavily in the north and southeast. Christians are prevalent in the south, particularly in Cotonou, the economic capital. It is not unusual for members of the same family to practice Christianity, Islam, traditional local religious beliefs, or a combination of all of these.

Human Rights

In April 1987, Amnesty International demanded that the government release 88 people who were illegally imprisoned and who, according to several sources, had been subjected to torture. Several of these had been involved in the student protests of 1985 or were suspected of being members of Parti Communiste du Dahoemy (PCD). The PCD was, at this time, a communist party in opposition to president Kérékou. They worked underground and membership of the organisation was punishable by law. In September 1993, the party became legal under the name of Parti Communiste du Benin (PCB).

Conférence Nationale des Forces Vives[12]

The gathering of such a "national conference for the forces of life" was to become an example for many other countries. It is such national conferences that are the most important common trait of the peaceful African regime shifts and the subsequent democratizations. In the same month similar meetings were announced in Congo, in March 1990 in Gabon, February 1991 in Zaïre, July and August of 1991 in Togo, July 1992 in Niger and in January 1993 in Chad.

But in Benin it didn't even proceed as the president had hoped for. Kérékou had misjudged the mood and situation. He hoped to be able to calm the delegates and continue as president. On 19 February 1990, 488 representatives from 50 oppositional groups gathered for a nine day conference in the largest city of the country, Cotonou. Led by President Kérékou, representatives from the government, several

---

12. Trasnlation by J.Johansen: National Congress for the Forces of Life

public authorities, the military, religious and political organizations and networks of different kinds had gathered (Nugent, 2004, p. 387). The attendees rejected the agenda that Kérékou had proposed right from the beginning and refused to accept him as chair of the meeting. Instead, they elected Archbishop Isidore de Souza to lead the conference. From that moment on the gathering would have major consequences for the African continent (Keesing's Record of World Events 1990, p. 37238). What followed has been described as a civil coup d'état. The same conference that Kérékou himself had planned with the goal of reconciliation and support for his political agenda declared itself sovereign and, in principle, removed the president of the country (Keesing's Record of World Events 1990, p. 37238). An interesting thing to note is that, just as when the Polish Union Solidarity negotiated with Minister of Interior Kiszczak in 1980, every word of the negotiations became public. From Cotonou everything was broadcast on both radio and television. It is known that some parts of the military that were still loyal to Kérékou wanted him to dissolve the conference, arrest those who had returned from exile and force economic reforms by military means. Those parts of the army that supported this line were mainly from the northern parts of the country or ex-Marxists. But the possibility that it would end in a bloodbath resulted in lack of support for this line. Every commentator has agreed to this analysis in retrospect. Several senior officers had clearly stated that they would not use violence against their fellow countrymen in Cotonou (Bratton and van de Walle, 1992, p. 424, Decalo, 1997, p. 55).

It was during the sixth day of the conference that the main issue was decided. It was the proposal that the conference was now to consider itself sovereign and have the power to execute the decisions it had arrived at (Laloupo, 1993, Nzouankeu, 1993, p. 44-45). What was initially a forum for discussion had now become the most important and powerful political organ of Benin. In order to avoid further confrontations it was decided that Kérékou would continue as interim president until free and secret elections could be held. He saw that this was the end and publicly apologized for the regrettable events during his presidency.[13] In addition to the divided army and the fear of a bloodbath, it has been suggested by several people that a World Bank delegation visiting Cotonou following the conference was a cause of the development. Violent clashes probably prevent the delegation

Members of the High Council of the Republic, formed in February 1990 to democratize the country. The council was chaired by Archbishop Isidore de Souza. Source: http://www.courconstitutionnelle-benin.org/hcr/presentation.html accessed: 1 Sept. 2017

from traveling back to Washington with a suggestion for increased support. In this context it should be noted that Nicéphore Soglo, who became interim Prime Minister, was a former employee of The World Bank and had full support from France. This indicates that external financial and political actors had an important role in the development of events. Even if they did not sit at the negotiation table, they obviously had an impact on the outcome.

An important factor to keep in mind is that Kérékou probably had greater interest in saving the country from chaos and collapse than, for example General Éyadéma in Togo. Kérékou has been described

---

13. In "Benin: Test-Tube Democracy", Anon, 1990. Benin: Test-Tube Democracy. *Africa Confidential* 31, 4-5. it is described as "the deplorable and regrettable incidents".

by many as a patriot who in many situations put the country before his own personal interests. He did not have the same personal involvement, and therefore responsibility, for many of the injustices that took place during his rule. He was also granted amnesty by the conference and therefore did not risk future trial and punishment.

In addition to these conciliatory traits, several authors have proposed the idea that the national conference can be seen as a form of revenge of Benin's civil society against president Kérékou. They had, on many occasions, opposed the regime on specific issues and also Kérékou personally. With some success, African leaders used three different strategies when protests became too massive. They had relented to economic demands by giving those who complained certain increases in salaries or other economic benefits. But Benin was poor, also in natural resources, and could not therefore revitalize the economy through such simple means. The fact that international lenders and donors decreased their support also made the situation worse.

The other tactic was to give representatives of those who complained positions inside the system, or to make other political concessions. This was used in situations where the economy did not allow meeting of the demands. At the end of 1989, President Kérékou gave several opposition members seats in the administration. In August, he appointed as finance minister the head of the legal faculty, in an attempt to face down the turbulence and the demands for his resignation (Heilbrunn, 1993, p. 286). In September, he abandoned Marxism-Leninism as the official policy of the state (Keesing's Record of World Events, 1989, p. 37115) and pardoned many imprisoned opposition figures.

The third tactic was to increase repression with police and military force (Bratton and van de Walle, 1992, p. 424). This required that the army and the police were loyal and that the threat of violence would lessen oppositional activity. The problem for the rulers was that brutal repression against demonstrators could backfire. This had led many rulers to lose political power completely.[14]

At the end of 1989, the Benin opposition forces were no longer focused on single issues. They stood together with the demand that the whole system needed to change (Bratton and van de Walle, 1992, p. 424). They had no more patience; this time they would not be satisfied with lesser changes of the regime's policies. It was exceptional and new that civil society stood up against a state on the African continent. A nonviolent strategy was the basis of this political experiment. We will return later in this text to the question of how deliberate or planned the strategy was.

As I have already mentioned, these actions inspired others to try the same strategy. But, as the developments in neighboring Togo west of Benin showed, it was no guarantee for success. In Zaïre and Gabon, the regimes also agreed to gather national conferences, but they did not manage to proclaim free elections or overthrow the regimes. Even if Togo, Zaïre and Gabon were unsuccessful, others continued with similar strategies and many managed to inspire important changes. The Republic of Congo and Nigeria are other examples where national conferences like these clearly had a decisive role in creating more democratic societies (Bratton and van de Walle, 1992, p. 423).

In Benin, it was mainly organizations and networks from the southern parts of the country that had built a force strong enough to challenge the regime. Furthermore, France had given clear signals that it would no longer support every former colony. Democratization, a functioning economy and less corruption were important criteria for support from Paris. During the June 1990 Franco-African summit in La Baule, France, President Mitterand declared that it was about time that former colonies started a process of democratization. He also said that not everyone represented in the national conference of Benin were good friends of the French state (Keesing's Record of World

---

14. See Martin (2007) for analysis and examples of the backfire effect.

Events 1990, p. 37524). This was a veiled confirmation that Kérékou could be removed without France interfering.

Furthermore, Houngnikpo (2001) argues that French double standards created the pressures and influence that mattered for how democratization played out differently in Benin and Togo:

> *France's policies until recently have revolved around the support of various autocrats. Now, however, Africa's corrupt and autocratic regimes face strong pressures from an indigenous civil society that France regards with suspicion, resulting in French policy that has grown inconsistent and dependent on the particular economic and political interests that France has at stake in countries involved (p. 51).*

In addition to this, "while France has supported democratic reforms in some countries it has turned a blind eye as reforms have stagnated in others." (p. 52). In summary, France was particularly concerned with encouraging the democratization of Benin and worked to achieve this result.

The introduction of a multi-party system in Benin was the beginning of something new. The first free elections in the country were held in 1991, this time with several political parties to choose from. Politics was still based to a large extent on ethnicity. But, as opposed to the tripartite power in the seventies, there were now many political opportunities and ethnic groups with their own leaders.

Civil Society in Benin

Civil society as a concept is difficult to define. In the African context it is even harder. It is difficult to find equivalents of the traditional popular movements of the Nordic countries in an African country like Benin. Zolberg (1968) wrote that Africa is "an almost institutionless arena with conflict and disorder as its most prominent features" (Zolberg, 1968, p. 70). Makumbe discusses in *International Affairs* whether one can talk about civil society in Africa at all (Makumbe, 1998, pp. 305-317). He writes that the colonial governments destroyed most of the civil groups and organizations that existed before the colonial era. These groups were seen as threats and as a potential basis for mobilization against colonial rule. During colonial times, there were also active policies with the goal of hindering the political influence of groups other than those that the colonial power trusted; these consisted almost exclusively of colonists. Africans were, in most cases, excluded from those organizations that existed. Makumbe ends his article with the conclusion that there exists a civil society in Africa, but that it has difficulty growing stronger (Makumbe, 1998, p. 316). The states have not been independent long enough to be able to create large and effective organizations.

In this chapter, the concept of "civil society" is used in its historical meaning, including basically all organized activity outside the state domain. An exception is groups using armed violence. This includes religious communities, private enterprises, professional organizations, trade unions, student organizations and oppositional parties. We have used this definition partly because the literature on political change in Benin uses a similar concept, and partly because it is well suited for our analysis as part the theoretical discussions.

Benin was to some degree different from many other African states. Almost unique was the fact that Benin had relatively strong organizations that were not under control of the authorities (Harbeson et al., 1994, Widner, 1994, Monga, 1995). These were organizations that represented social, religious, professional and political interests (Makumbe, 1998, p. 308). It was when these civil society movements agreed on gathering their forces to end twenty years of President Kérékou's authoritarian rule that the opposition gained power to challenge the regime. Their primary demand was that all large oppositional groups be allowed to send representatives to a conference, including those groups that had left the country for political reasons. This conference should be empowered to discuss present grievances and suggest political reforms. Subsequently, free elections were to be held.

Kérékou agreed to this in the hope of arriving at a reconciliation and acceptance of the harsh economic austerity measures that were necessary to save the financial system. The country had been forced to give in to the strict demands from global financial institutions which would not be accepted by the opposition.

The division of Africa by European colonizers did not make it easier for the new born countries to function properly after independence. Traditional ethnic and cultural unities were often fragmented,

The seat of the National Assembly of Benin

while many states suffered from actually consisting of a mosaic of cultures, languages, religions and traditions. The fact that most of the African states were liberated with guerilla warfare as the dominant method of struggle meant that new leaders were recruited from the ranks of Marxists guerillas. Their training, upbringing, experience, knowledge, language and even custom of clothes were dominated by warfare, military structures and military ways of thought. Amanda Peralta describes a similar experience from her struggle in Argentina (Peralta, 1990), and much of the discussion is just as important in an African context. The outcomes for the African states were, with few exceptions, communist one-party states with limited democratic rights and freedoms.

Who created the alliance that brought the demand of a national conference and free elections in Benin? As in many other African countries, it was mainly university students who drove the struggle that would lead to democratization. Their difficult and worsening conditions as students made them willing to move into the streets in protest, going on strikes and demonstrating. The students had been on strike and demonstrated already in 1985, and from January 1989 they were on strike for several months. In March, 401 teachers were fired for taking part in the strikes.[15]

A splinter group from the state approved national union, Union nationale de syndicats des travailleurs du Bénin (UNSTB) was formed. They took the name Coopérative Universitaire des Etudiants du Bénin (CUEB). Others had been part of the authoritarian Fédération des étudiantes d'Afrique noire en France (FEANF), an organization that many broke from and created Union générale des étudiantes et élèves du Dahomey (UGEED), an underground organization that became public when the regime shift was confirmed (Heilbrunn, 1993, p. 292).

The worsened situation that the students directly experienced was part of the "structural adjustment program" that the World Bank and others hade demanded in return for loans to Benin (Nkinyangi, 1991).

---

15. <http://www.whirledbank.org/development/sap.html>, accessed 2008-04-26

In April 1986, it was decided that salaries for government employees were to be cut by 10%, to satisfy demands from the IMF that the government had accepted in order to get stability loans (Heilbrunn, 1993, p. 283). These miserable economic circumstances were the cause of the first student actions at the end of the eighties. The students were also first on the scene when the situation became more critical during the fall of 1989 (Bratton and Van de Walle, 1997). Later, the students presented more political demands. We can see parallels to Solidarity in Poland here as well. Their demands went from economic to political as they achieved success, were strengthened and grew (Cirtautas, 1997). In Benin many students had attended Soviet universities, others French universities and colleges. The contact that the well-educated class had with the rest of the world was clearly an important source of knowledge of global events at the end of the eighties, especially 1989. The fall of the Berlin Wall was naturally an important event also in Benin. The fact that a country that called itself communist and had a personality cult around its leader could still remove them, like in Nicolae Ceausescu's Romania, showed inspiring possibilities.

Even if there was little international news in the state media, students and people with higher education had access to news through the weekly Jeune Afrique and the radio station Radio France Internationale (Bratton and van de Walle, 1992, p. 431). There is no doubt that the events in the rest of the world in the turbulent year of 1989 worked as a catalyst for the events in Benin. When ex-president Julius Nyere of Tanzania returned from a visit to East German Leipzig, the center for the demonstrations against the communist regime, and publicly stated that one party-systems were no longer "holy" it fueled debate on the entire African continent, including Benin (Bratton and van de Walle, 1992, p. 431).

It is interesting to note that Monga identifies four key groups that matter for civil society's self-managment and that drive its attempt to "re-kindle social consciences": students, clergy, lawyers, as well as intellectuals and journalists (Célestin 1995, p. 366). In Benin it was largely students and the clergy that initially took this role.

However, in addition to the majority of students, large groups of "youth" and unemployed took part in the protests as well. We use quotes around "youth" here because it was not their specific age that is significant. It refers to groups that had not been able to enter adult life because of marginalization. Nwakiaku cites Achille Mbembe with the expression "the politics of the belly", and argues that these demands should not be differentiated from the democratic demands of students, teachers, lawyers and political activists (Nwajiaku, 1994, p. 436). Another part of civil society participating in the protests were commercial actors and professional organizations. Africa has of course always had organizations working to improve conditions of life for their members. In the modern era, Benin has had organizations such as Association Professionnelle de Revendeuses de Tissu (APRT) and Union Nationale des Commerçantes du Bénin (UNACOBE). The latter was close to the government when it was funded in 1976 and gathered many local businessmen in a countrywide organization (Heilbrunn, 1997, p. 478). Both organizations already supported the democratic demands at the beginning of the democratic movement (Nwajiaku, 1994, p. 433). They saw the possibilities to improve economic development as the most important effect of a regime change. Every organization worked in their specific fashion. Their struggle for democracy was dependent on the individual organization, its structure, social basis and relation to the state (Heilbrunn, 1997, p. 473). All the women from Togo that went under the name of Nana Benz conducted currency exchange and had business with colleagues in

Benin. Many even lived in both countries (Heilbrunn, 1997, p. 474). They had "sisters" in Benin who were also strong and independent women. Many became members of UNACOBE, and their relative independence was supported by the organization. They were strong advocates for democracy, a multi-party system and more transparency in Benin and Togo. When the banking system collapsed, UNACOBE revoked all its support of president Kérékou and, together with two other organizations, formed the women's organization Organisation des Femmes Entrepreneurs et Commerçantes de l'Afrique de l'Ouest (OFECAO)[16].

Different from Togo, most organizations in Benin were decentralized and had a greater distance from state politics. An example is UNACOBE which had a regional structure in each of the

Union National Des Conduceurs Du Benin

six provinces, where each region had significant autonomy. They had great legitimacy defending local merchants from foreign competition. This is also an important explanation for why they grew stronger during the democratization process. Many of UNACOBE's leaders

---

16. Heilbrunn, (1993) Social Origins of National Conferences in Benin and Togo. *Journal of Modern African Studies.*

were also active in religious networks in the Vodou, Christian and Muslim congregations (Heilbrunn, 1997, p. 482). Their network, cooperation and continuous communication were decisive factors in the democratic movement. They played important roles during the Conférence Nationale des Forces Vives and later in the new regime (Heilbrunn, 1997, p. 474).

They demanded a new constitution, a multi-party system, liberalization of economic policy, an end to structural rationalization, freedom of association, right to strike, increased grants for students and improvements in university infrastructure (Nwajiaku, 1994, p. 435). In August 1989, teachers in the Syndicat des Enseignants du Supérieur (SYNES Union)[17] decided to join students and workers in the struggle for increased democracy. UNSTB, which was controlled by the regime, had at the time of the national conference lost the majority of its members (Nwajiaku, 1994, p. 435). During the first two weeks of 1990, a number of free unions were formed. One of these new unions was Syndicat National des Travailleurs des Postes et Télécommunicationes, SYNAPOSTEL, which in January 1990 demanded rights to strike, free unions and representation in the delegation that negotiated with the World Bank. In the beginning they were secret and worked underground, but later they struggled in the open against the one-party state (Heilbrunn, 1993, p. 284). Many of the leaders of the new unions had been working for a long time in UNSTB, but were among those shut out from wage negotiations and other economic issues.

In July 1989, the chairman of the Lawyer's Union, René Ahouansou, and the head of the legal faculty at Université Nationale du Bénin, Robert Dossou, presented a list of demands for political reform. It was delivered to President Kérékou and contained demands that the dominant party should renounce much of the monopoly and power it had in different parts of society. There were also demands for a general amnesty for political prisoners and that the repression against striking

---

17. This union was formed by an outbreak from UNSTB.

teachers had to stop. They argued that this was important to prevent violent riots in the country (Heilbrunn, 1993, p. 285).

The fourth aspect of civil society in Benin that played an important role in the critical phace leading up to the national coalition in February 1990 were the religious organizations and networks. As stated previously, the population contains a diverse mix of religions. No single religion dominates the whole country. Colonialism and subsequent missionary activity had resulted in 42% of the population being Christian and close to 25% being Muslim. The traditional religions, with Vodou dominating, were still practiced by 24% of the population. The different religious communities are organized in congregations and similar structures and meet regularly. It has been difficult to find good documentation on the exact role of these communities during the revolutionary processes that led up to the national conference, but many show that they did participate. It is a reasonable hypothesis that they were important information channels. At their meetings and gatherings, or in connection to them news spread, events were discussed and possibly decisions were made about participating in actions of different kinds. Ranger thoroughly discusses the role of religious movements in African politics south of Sahara (Ranger, 1986). Even if Ranger does not discuss Benin specifically, it is obvious that Christians, Muslims and traditional religions played an important role in the political agenda. Religious leaders were respected in Benin just as in other countries.[18]

Information and Communication

Media became important during the last years before the national conference. 1988 Kérekou lifted the strict state censure and many new publications, fiercely critical of the regime, appeared. In March 1988 in Cotonou, La Gazette du Golfe started publication and,

---

18. A more thorough analysis of the role of the Christian Church in revolutions since the French in 1789, up until the revolutions in Latin America in the seventies, can be found in Houtart & Rousseau, (1971).

three months later, Tam-Tam Express (Gbado, 1990, p. 10). They led the opposition forward with their views and created an arena for spreading and discussing the critique. They also transmitted news of the important revolutionary events in the rest of the world. But in a small country with widespread illiteracy other media was more important than newspapers and journals.

After the decolonization of Africa south of the Sahara the number of radio stations increased tremendously. In 1960 there were 252 radio stations, while fifteen years later there were 458. Even more important is the fact that in 1965 there existed 23 radio receivers per 1000 people, increasing to 164 per 1000 in 1984 (Nugent, 2004, p. 382). UNESCO worked actively on giving the population outside the larger cities access to radio. The major international radio and television networks like CNN, BBC World Service, Voice of America and Radio France Internationale were the most important sources providing insight on current political events abroad. Under the one party regime, censorship was widespread and much news was never reported. It was common practice for government ministers to not make any appearance in domestic media, but agree to interviews in international media where they rebutted the allegations of the opposition. This implied that they saw the international arena as more important than the domestic and internal debate. During the same period as the national conferences, more and more private radio stations appeared. Even during the years of harshest repression there existed a phenomena in the cities under the name radio trottoir (pavement radio). It consisted of rumors and stories that were spread through word of mouth in marketplaces and other places where people met. Private newspapers often relayed this "news". This gave them greater legitimacy, since they were written "black on white". James Scott in his books *Weapons of the Weak* (Scott, 1985) and *Domination and the Art of Resistance* (Scott, 1990) shows the effect and weight of these types of subcultural forms of resistance and communication. Scott bases his works on empirical research from Asia, but it is nonetheless possible to draw general conclusions from the research. It was also common that private newspapers spread stories that later were taken up by radio trottoir (Nugent 2004, p. 384). This created a two way channel in Benin between printed media and the discussions of people in the street and in private. It was not only possibile to write articles or letters from the reader, but the newspapers also actively searched for and relayed the discussions taking place on pavements and in town squares.

In other words, the communication opportunities were decisive in giving the opposition a way to organize and discuss its goals and strategies.

Reasons for the Protest, Sources of Inspiration and Results

Benin was no isolated event in French speaking Africa. According to Bratton and Van De Walle, the yearly British publication Africa South of Asahara mentioned seventeen large scale political protests in Benin from 1985 through 1994 (Bratton and Van de Walle, 1997, pp. 286-287). This makes Benin one of the African countries with the most political protests during this period. Strikes and demonstrations dominated the political mass protests. Most of the political activity took place in the cities, but many in the countryside also took part in the strikes.

Bratton and Van De Walle have identified the four most important factors explaining the causes of political protests in Africa. They can be arranged according to importance, as follows:

1. Competition within the civil society (measured by numbers of active trade unions in the country);

2. Political activity (measured by number of elections during the post colonial period);

3. Number of neighboring countries with the same colonial background;

4. Number of Structural Adjustment Programs (Bratton and Van de Walle, 1997, p. 150-151).

They focused on Africa as a whole and its relevance to Benin is debateable. But, as we saw earlier, the number of unions increased heavily during the period leading up to the national conference. In terms of the number of elections, Benin could not show that many. During President Kérékou's rule, the Marxist-Leninist regime did not bother with holding elections. However, when the Revolutionary Military Council was dissolved in 1979, parliamentary elections were held. There were also parliamentary elections in 1984 and 1989. However, there were no presidential elections between 1970 and 1991, when the national conference declared one. Of neighboring Togo, Burkina Faso, Niger and Nigeria, the first three were French colonies. Here is a clear correlation with Bratton and Van De Walle's investigation. Concerning the fourth factor, the number of Structural Adjustment Programs, it is obvious that these programs were seen as an important cause of the worsened economic conditions. In summary, the general results for Africa seem to fit the Benin situation quite well.

Many have claimed that the economic factors behind the changes were the most important. It is obvious that all countries where democratization took place through national conferences had economic problems. It is also a fact that many of the protests started out as reactions against miserable economic conditions. However, there are many countries that have had similar and far worse economic conditions without them leading to demands for national conferences or any other type of democratization. We have not seen examples of similar processes on the African continent without a history of economic problems. Nor have we seen many examples of blooming economies in Africa south of Sahara during the first decades after decolonization.

Bad economic conditions are an important and maybe even necessary factor for starting the process, but it is not enough of an explanation in itself. In a discussion on the role of the economy one also has to include a class perspective, where one analyzes which class in society a) faces economic hardships and b) takes initiative to protest. It is well known that the poorest rarely have surplus resources, time and initiative to lead protests. It is also probable that the limit of a "tolerable" economic situation for the educated middle class is a more important factor than the same for the lowest classes. If the middle class no longer receives the standard of life they expect they participate in a revolt, even if they are far better off than the poorest in society. It is the difference between expected development and actual development that is the decisive factor. Tedd Gurr in *Why Men Rebel* has described in detail how relative deprivation can be used as an indicator on the likelihood of a revolt (Gurr, 1970).

Another explanation for the revolts is that large parts of Africa have a tradition of showing discontent in times of trouble. Protests, strikes, boycotts, demonstrations and revolts have frequently been used by teachers, students, public employees and other workers throughout the post-colonial period. In French speaking countries like Congo, Mali, Cote d'Ivoire and Senegal, open confrontations have been common. The same goes for English speaking countries like Kenya, Zambia and South Africa. In Sudan, president Nimiery was forced to resign after large protests in 1985. There is, in other words, nothing exceptional about the fact that people protest when they are discontent. The unique aspect of the events of 1989 and onwards in the French speaking countries was that the demands were not only for the regime to step down, but for national conferences to take place. This contains an unusual constructive element where the intent was to enable a majority of the citizens of the country to take part in an open debate on what needed to be done. The demands for these kinds of conferences are a qualitatively new dimension of the history of revolutionary movements. This is a new invention in strategies for national liberation. To be inclusive and constructive is something completely different from armed revolutionary struggles to take power and put authoritarian regimes in place. It is possible that we can see the first grains of what would later happen in South Africa, where Nelson Mandela allowed the old apartheid representatives to be a part of the first ANC government.

In one of the few overviews of the history and present situation of trade unions in West Africa, Phelan (2011) emphasises the important role played by the trade unions in West Africa already in the independence struggles, but also within the newly independent states and the struggle against authoritarianism, the struggle against the policies and adverse effects of the structural adjustment programmes, as well as during the democratic transitions. This is despite the fact that the number of wage workers was relatively small (4-5 % of the population in West Africa, p. 10) and trade unionism was imported from the colonial centres. Phelan (2011, p. 4) argues that West Africa is a strong example of what is today called "social movement unionism", i.e. broad social alliances of movements and trade unions, where "trade unions were part of larger movements of resistance and change" (p. 5). The heritage of nation building and the relative absence of white settler colonialism, some scholars suggest, provided fertile ground for the potent intellectual and political currents that fuelled anti-colonial sentiment and trade union development. Among the West African states, all former British colonies and only one former French colony, Benin, established a multiparty government. However, it lasted only twelve years and, during that short period, there were no less than twelve attempts for "coups d'état, of which five were successful" (Imorou 2011: 133). Subsequently, "West Africa became known as 'the coup d'état belt' of Africa. Since 1963, every country in West Africa with the exception of Senegal has experienced coups d'état and direct military rule" (Phelan 2011:9). Kérékou and the Marxist-Leninist regime disbanded several trade union federations and created a state-controlled national federation in 1974 (p. 11). Despite this, "the spirit if not the structure of independent unionism remained, and thus workers and their unions were able to play a leading role in the pro-democracy movement" (p. 11). Since the 1970s economic crisis and the quadrupled oil price, West African countries developed external debt of "at least fifty per cent of its GDP", and in Benin it was even worse (p. 13). According to UNDP surveys, during the 1980s and 1990s Benin belonged to the world's poorest countries (p. 14). Despite that the structural adjustment programmes having a "deleterious impact on West African trade unions" (p. 14), it was "coalitions of trade unions, student unions and other civil society actors in the forefront of movements for political liberalisation in the late 1980s and early 1990s" (p. 15). "A pro-democracy wave swept across sub-Saharan Africa … first appearing in Benin in 1989" (p. 15), and taken up firstly in Mali 1990, then in Togo 1991 and Ghana 1992 (pp. 16-17). Phelan argues that "the underlying causes of the democratic wave were the privations created by years of austerity under IMF sponsored structural adjustment and the loss of legitimacy experienced by authoritarian regimes after years of repression, corruption and dismal economic performance" (p. 16). In the 1980s Benin was drawn into structural adjustment, despite still having a Marxist regime. To Phelan it was the "financial constraints" together with "public disenchantment" that led to "political paralysis and a crisis of legitimacy" for the regime, a situation which could not be dealt with like before; with effective state repression (p. 16).

Consequently, the events in Benin were to have enormous consequences on the whole continent. It should be noted that the strategy was not always a success. In the same way that every political tool or strategy can fail, there were also attempts here that did not succeed. One reason was that many leaders of authoritarian regimes saw what had happened in Benin and did all they could to avoid similar outcomes. In Congo, President Sassou-Nguesso refused to take part in a national conference. It was only after the defense chief had declared himself neutral in relation to the internal conflicts and been unwilling to use soldiers against the striking workers that he accepted the demand (Bratton and Van de Walle, 1997, p. 173).

Seven cases of "Conférences nationales"

On the other hand, as mentioned above, it can be said that France had a major part to play in the success or failure of revolutions. Nwajiaku, (1994) claims that seven "Conférences nationales" took place in Francophone Africa between Feb 1990 and Jan 1993: **Benin** and **Republic of Congo,** Feb. 90, **Gabon**, March 90, **Zaïre**, Feb. 91, **Togo**, July/Aug. 91, **Niger**, July 92, and **Chad**, Jan 93. (p. 449, note 1). All of these are under-reseaerched. Nwajiaku argues that the policy of France mattered a lot for the differences between the countries;

> "by way of contrast, Kérékou did not enjoy the same degree of support from France or her international finance partners. Until 1980, the Marxist-Leninist years had largely isolated Benin from Western assistance. In any case, possessing few natural resources, the country lacked the necessary leverage with which to secure development assistance from international donors." (p. 431).

> "In 1989, Kérékou's position as head of an effectively bankrupt state, in which the networks of his former patrimonial base had collapsed, meant that he was forced to accept the sovereignty of the CN [Conférences nationales], isolated as he was from the [ruling party, PRPB], as well as the army, and under pressure from France to break the political and economic deadlock. On the other hand, during 1990-1, Eyadéma's control of the army, the assured loyalty

of the members of the [ruling party, RPT], and the relatively intact nature of his networks of political power, enabled him to subvert the authority of the CN." (p. 431).

It is uncertain how prepared civil society was before they acted. There is no documentation to prove that the Benin opposition had planned

The 2018 28th anniversary of the Conference of the Forces of the Beninese Nation in February 1990.

their actions over the long term. Training and practical exercises in civil disobedience are not documented either. This does not necessarily mean that it did not take place, but our assessment is that it probably did not. As mentioned above, lots of inspiration was drawn from other countries, both historical and contemporary, but no direct forms of cooperation or exchange of strategies can be proven. That the idea of nonviolence had been spread around the world and developed in different contexts is not unknown, it is thoroughly treated in chapter three of Stellan Vinthagen's book *Ickevåldsaktion* (Vinthagen,

2005, pp. 105-153). However, in the case of Benin it was probably more on the idea level and less on the practical aspect of exchanging experiences. Most information probably came from the media and not from individuals or groups that had fought for democracy in other countries.

Additionally, Even if there are no roots reaching back to the independence struggle in India there are clear parallels to Gandhi's wish for a common state for Hindus, Muslims and the British when the British colony was liberated (Ashe, 1968, pp. 353-385). However, Gandhi's project failed whereas the wave of national conferences and democratization processes that took place in Africa during the nineties was far more successful in maintaining national unity. These countries were not divided like India. But not all should be glorified. Zaire (Democratic Republic of the Congo) are in the midst of serious domestic and international conflicts.

Gandhi is also relevant when discussing the inspiration from other countries that played a role in Benin. The fact that Gandhi began his work against oppression and towards ethical and sustainable societies during his years in South Africa (Pyarelal, 1980, Pyarelal, 1986, Nayar, 1989)[19] is hardly an important factor for the developments in Benin. However, it is likely that many of those inspired by Gandhi who worked for freedom and democracy in the US (Martin Luther King), in Eastern Europe (Lech Walesa and Vaclav Havel), Philippines (Corazon Aquino) or the students at Tiananmen Square in Beijing had an effect on the well educated in Benin. Benin had a relatively high number of students and they did not live in a vacuum. Political history was part of the ongoing discussions. It is also possible that Kwame Nkhruma in Ghana and the struggle they fought against the British colonial empire was an important inspiration. However, the

---

19. This period of Gandhi's life and the work that he did in South Africa is well described by Shri Pyarelal in volume II, III, IV of the biography Mahatma Gandhi. Volume IV was finished by Sushila Nayar after Shri Pyarelal passed away.

language barrier between French and English speakers could have been an issue. As we mentioned above, the many revolutionary events in the communist countries during 1989 were important themes having an impact on the Benin context. The fall of the Berlin wall was of course just as important an event in Marxist-Leninist Benin as it was everywhere else in the world. The fact that it was possible to change an authoritarian regime was probably the most important message. No cases of transferred strategic ideas or other forms of direct contact between Eastern Europe and Benin have been found. This does not necessarily mean that there have been none, but they are not known in the literature.

We rely on neither structure nor agency in order to explain the transition, but on a combination of both. Moreover, we argue it is neither general structures such as "capitalism", "modernism", "colonialism", the "regime" (Foran 2005; Goodwin 1988?; Skocpol 1979; etc.), nor strategic excellence of individual actors (Ackerman & DuVall 2000, Chenoweth & Stephan 2011) that decides the occurrences, trajectories or outcomes of protests in revolutionary transitions and regime changes such as in Benin 1989-90. We claim the conflictual interaction between actors in a particular context is what matters (Bratton & van de Walle 1997; McAdam, Tarrow and Tilly 2001; Nepstad 2011; Roberts and Ash 2009; Schock 2005). More specifically, it is the existing institutional conditions (institutional actors of the state and civil society, possible alliances, etc.) and heritage (previous experience of participation, protests, politics, etc.) that matter for how the protests are formed, their frequency and resilience and, furthermore, the prevalent mechanisms inherent in the interaction dynamics between institutionally established as well as newly formed actors, which ultimately decides the outcome.

Thus, the strategy of actors does matter, but strategy is mediated through existing institutional conditions and prevalent interaction mechanisms. In order to be successful, any strategy applied by actors has to skillfully navigate given established rules (i.e. institutions) within a certain context (politics, culture, economy). Contexts are inherently local, yet always more or less influenced from outside. Intelligent plans of action will remain in the mind of someone without being applied or activated within a grievance group if that individual does not, at least, to some fundamental degree, conform to how actions are commonly conducted in that context and group. Simultaneously, strategies are not mechanical repetitions of historic repertoires but need to motivate participants with convincing new variations and applications. Strategies need to explain in a reasonable way why it makes sense (within that tradition of politics) to act now and in a particular way. Similarly, action repertoires that get mobilized will not be understood if they do not adapt to some degree to the rules of the interaction game played by other actors in that context. Furthermore, they will not be successful if they do not also break some of the expectations of other actors by being more innovative or resilient than others. Challenges, surprises and "smart moves" are creative combinations of knowing the political game and innovating it.

Taken together, we claim strategies have to be rooted in the context in which they arise, and at the same time have to deviate somewhat from what was done last time. If challengers manage to make such a creative use of the contextual conditions they stand a chance to engage networks of subalterns and overcome competitors in a strive towards social change.

The peaceful methodology obviously has a great impact on the result. Strikes, demonstrations, boycotts and other forms of protest have a completely different effect than violent means such as guerilla warfare. Open protests are less elitist than wars where only the physically able and armed can participate. Demonstrations on streets and squares can gather everyone able to move in a public space. Peaceful means also create less conflict than means involving violence. Violence and killing, on a small or large scale, often breeds new conflicts in the future. Survivors and their representatives have a tendency to want to "hit back" against the perpetrators of violence. This "justified violence" is mostly a theoretical concept. The victims and their friends and relatives cannot see the justice in the loss of a loved one. Violence hurts all the roles that a person has. The policewoman can also be a mother, chess player, union activist, lover, daughter and neighbor. If she is killed all these roles are taken from her. Here nonviolence shows one of its largest advantages: it can be directed at a specific role a person plays and is therefore far more exact and precise than the always brutal violence. During the period after the peaceful revolution, Benin had far fewer conflicts than what would probably have been the case if the upheavals were bathed in blood.

In addition to this, (Abrahamsen, 1997) argues that there is a combined dynamic between internal and external factors behind the democratization in Sub-Saharan Africa: "Internal and external causes are interlinked and intertwined in such complex ways that what at first glance appears to be internal may on closer inspection reveal strong external influences." (p. 129). He states that:

> *"Two closely related internal causes of democratisation have been presented in contemporary literature: economic decline and a crisis of legitimacy" (p. 133). "In fact, the economic crisis and the lack of legitimacy identified as the domestic causes of democratisation cannot be divorced from externally imposed adjustment programmes" (p. 141).*
>
> *"The claim that external factors are only of an inspirational, supportive character amounts to an implicit acceptance of attempts by the IFIs [International Financial Institutions], and in particular the World Bank, to absolve themselves from any responsibility for Africa's economic failure and to present their policy prescriptions as a set of technical truths. A perception of the IFIs as neutral and technocratic, as opposed to ideological and political, permeates conventional scholarship" (p. 144).*
>
> *"Donors and creditors have explained the failure of SAPs [Structural*

Adjustment Programmes] to generate growth on the African continent by asserting that political factors, or 'poor governance', stood in the way of the 'right' economic policies. In the words of the World Bank, 'a crisis of governance' underlies the 'litany of Africa's development problems' (p. 146).

"It is bordering on the political naïve to treat the political and economic ideas emanating from donors and creditors as neutral and merely technocratic. This, however, is the logical conclusion of statements which assert that international factors have been merely inspirational and supportive of political change. But donors and creditors are not disinterested, detached observers of world events. They do not seek simply to understand and describe the world, but to actively shape it in their image and to maintain the hegemonic world order" (p. 146).

Another external actor that was often seen as an important player in many of the irregular regime shifts towards the end of the eighties was the Catholic Church lead by Polish Pope John Paul II. In countries such as the Philippines (Bonner, 1987, p. 414, Schirmer and Shalom, 1987, pp. 250-252), Poland (Ash, 1991, pp. 107-109, 213-217 and 239-241) and Bolivia it is well known that the church played an important role inspiring and giving moral support to the opposition. To what degree they helped with other forms of support is not known. It is not unlikely that there was both economic support and transfer of knowledge. Liberation theology with its radical politics was also represented on the African continent. The fact that Catholic Arch Bishop Isidore de Souza was appointed to lead the national conference implies that the church and its representatives enjoyed great confidence in Benin.

According to an article in Time magazine by Lisa Beyer[20], the proposal for a national conference was presented to president Kérékou

---

20. <http://www.time.com/time/magazine/article/0,9171,970130,00.html>, Accessed 2008-04-26

in a memorandum by the French ambassador in December 1989. Specific constitutional changes were proposed in this memorandum. According to the article, Kérékou followed the recommendations almost without exception. In exchange, "considerable" support in the form of aid was promised. Beyer also cites the French cooperation and development minister Jacques Pelletier: "The wind that blows in the east should not be stopped in the south". Whether the proposition originated in Paris or whether it was the opposition that had whispered in France's ear we do not know. Others have pointed out that many traditional African societies (including Benin) have a tradition of gathering "village councils", where diverging views can be expressed and discussed, with common solutions found" (Bratton and Van de Walle, 1997, p. 172). The idea might have come from Paris, inspired by the events in 1789 and at the same time been well received since as a form of conflict management that the Benin population was familiar with.

Benin inaugurated what might be described as the 'national conference movement' in February 1990. Among the countries that followed suit were Congo and Togo. Heilbrunn (1993) argues that the different development and institutional traditions of the civil society in Benin and Togo explain the different outcomes of the struggles, and the different roles of their key instrument: a national conference. Accordingly, "the national conferences ... have invariably been organised by prominent professionals and leaders of trade unions" (p. 277). Despite otherwise striking similarities between the struggles for democracy in Benin and Togo, the results of the national conferences were dramatically different. Heilbrunn (1993) argues that in "Benin politicised groups were able to prepare for the national conference and ensure its outcome", while such groups were absent in Togo (p. 298). In Benin civil society groups "have always exerted political influence", and during the build up to the national conference not only broad agreements between diverse kinds of groups were possible, but also coalitions that pursued "national rather than ethno-regional interests", while civil society groups were "easily divided" in Togo (p. 298).

In any case, the conference came to form a significant part of the process. As we have observed many times before, it is difficult to create a strong enough opposition if the different oppositional elements are unable to cooperate and unite to form a single front. In Serbia 2000, Georgia 2003 and Ukraine 2004 it was decisive that the opposition had left their internal difficulties and stood united. Most regimes can handle a divided opposition relatively easily. At the conference this unity was obvious: when the president was ousted as chair of the conference; when Isisdore de Souza was unanimously chosen instead; when the conference appointed itself the highest authority in the country; when free elections for parliament and president were declared and that there would be a referendum on the new constitution, and that all decisions were to be implemented.

Conclusions

Based on the complex picture of the history leading up to, and the realization of, the national conference in Benin that we have described, it is nevertheless too early to draw any certain conclusion on cause and effect among the many factors, events and contexts that are relevant. And as Thomas Bierschenk (2018) argue; Benin has been democratizised but is still behind in developement. The outcome from a longer perspective is of course another important question to discuss. More research is needed.

Some of it is complete but, for example, a deeper study of the nonviolent means that the opposition used is missing. What have been written until now has not been focused on the influence of means on the development and the result. Many of the contextual factors has been discussed and some of the external actors have been analyzed. But a study providing an overall analysis of the different elements is missing.

Charles Tilly emphasizes the importance of coalitions and argues that social movements contribute to democratization when they fulfill the following criteria:

I totally agree that coalitions are necessary, but there are more variables that must be included in order to explain social movements positive contribution to the democratization of states (Tilly, 2004, p. 142-143).

We will now briefly discuss how such an analysis can be made. The starting point is that factors can be divided into a) important, b) necessary, c) sufficient, d) counter productive and e) irrelevant elements. Factors that have played an important role in the development of events, but which are not necessary for the result, are placed in the first group; possibly, the demand for a united opposition with common demands can be placed here. Factors that have impacted the process in a significant manner can be placed in group "b". Much indicates that the difficult economic situation during the eighties is such a factor, but it could be the change in situation, rather than the situation in itself, that was decisive. It is possible that two objectively similar situations are perceived differently depending on recent improvements or deterioration. As we have pointed out above, it is important to include a class perspective in the analysis. Factors that have not only been important and necessary for change, but even sufficient in themselves, can be placed in group "c". It is possible that there are no such single factors, but it should be included as a possibility. In the debate concerning external funding of the movements in Serbia, Georgia and Ukraine, suggestions have been made that the financial support from American actors was the decisive factor for the result. No one has presented strong empirical evidence for this, but the debate continues. Group "d" includes those kinds of factors that have an impact contrary to the intention. One typical example could be if an opposition group receives financial support from abroad and the authorities successfully label them puppets of a foreign actor. Another is violent actions that backfire. In category "e" you will find all the types of activities that have minimal, if any, impact on the situation. Without any empirical support, our qualified guess is that there are more of this type than what many donors/supporters, stakeholders and recipients will confess. Mapping support and outcome for different forms of external support during the three phases presented in the table below would help us to better understand the relationship.

	Initial phase	Peak phase	Post phase
A. Important factors			
B. Necessary factors			
C. Sufficient factors			
D. Counter productive factors			
E. Irrelevant factors			

Table 1: Three phases and five types of factors based on a similar tool for analyzing external support (Johansen, 2010).

Another set of variables necessary for this kind of analysis is during which phase of the process these factors function. Here, it might be practical to divide it into three consecutive stages: The initial, concerning preparations and background. After that there is implementation, which means the escalating part of the process when the decisive events take place; the result, in other words the changes that actually form the outcome. Important variables in one phase could have less importance in another. If a comparative analysis of a large number of empirical examples is conducted, it is likely that patterns will emerge that can lead towards more solid theories concerning the functions of social movements on state-level democratization processes. It might also be interesting to determine the correlation between the level of internal democracy within social movements and the level of democratization that is the result of their political impact on society.

When compiling the result, it is important to undertake the analysis from different time perspectives. What is celebrated as a victory can feel like a bad solution a few weeks, months or years later. Once again it is important to keep a class, gender and age perspective during the analysis. The upper class and a growing middle class can be very content, while poor senior citizens, unemployed people and students want the "good old days" back. Women are in a different situation than men, while younger and older people have different needs. Almost all countries that have gone through peaceful revolutions have shortly thereafter imposed a neoliberal market economy where the role of the state is heavily reduced. This is probably the best system for increasing growth created by man. However, it totally lacks mechanisms for distribution of wealth. This results in greater class differences in economies following neoliberal principles and values.

To measure the result it is essential to have a notion of the expectations. Many peaceful revolutions have been focused on expectations on what one did not want, for example not wanting the current regime or certain politicians to lead the country. In Benin, there were far more explicit and constructive wishes for the future. Freedom of speech, general and free elections, a multi-party system, the right to strike, freedom of association and so forth, were demands presented during the national conference. And this was what was realized when the conference took power in its own hands. In the economic sphere, it was less clear what the demands were other than a better economic situation for the people. That market liberalism was to rule was not clearly pronounced. The negative consequences of this system, as far as the literature shows, are not part of the debate either.

On one level, this review of democratization in Benin can tell us something about the preparation and implementation of resistance against the authoritarian regime. But one should not draw far-reaching conclusions. One should be careful, since it is only a single case. These are complex processes where many parts are far from sufficiently researched. The Benin example nonetheless shows a different kind of resistance compared to the peaceful revolutions in Poland 1980-89, Philippines 1986 or Serbia 2000. During a central phase of the struggle in Benin, the resistance took the form of the opposition inviting the formal authorities to discussions; this took place altogether on the terms of the opposition. Discussions also took place in most other examples of peaceful transfers of rule and democratization processes, but in Benin the alliance was broader than usual and therefore stronger. The constructive path showed good results and built the groundwork for a future united state. This reminds us of what Nelson Mandela did four years later when ANC, after its landslide victory, invited representatives of the white minority to take part in the government during the first term. Not because they had to, but for reconciliation and building a common future for all citizens. In both these cases, a form of resistance less marked by traditional power relations and more by wisdom, a view to the future and good insights into sensible conflict management can be observed. Of course, they are based on a power relation, but the power is not used to fight and humiliate the antagonist. The power is used to decide how the changes are to be made. It is as much about the process as the goal.

The Benin example should be studied in more detail. The same goes for the other cases of irregular regime shifts in Africa. Much research remains to be done before we have a good understanding of these revolutionary events. If we want to learn how to manage these national conflicts concerning government, democracy and the inclusion of minorities, we should study the best examples. Benin is a good place to start.

References

Abrahamian, E., 1982. *Iran between two revolutions.* Princeton, N.J.: Princeton University Press.

Ackerman, P. and J. DuVall (2000). *A force more powerful: a century of nonviolent conflict.* New York, St. Martin's Press.

Anon, 1990. Benin: Test-Tube Democracy. *Africa Confidential,* 31, 4-5.

Arjomand, S.A., 1988. *The turban for the crown : the Islamic revolution in Iran.* New York: Oxford University Press.

Ash, T.G., 1991. *The Polish revolution: Solidarity.* Rev. and updated ed. London: Granta Books.

Ashe, G., 1968. *Gandhi*. New York: Stein and Day.

Åslund, A. & Mcfaul, M., 2006. *Revolution in orange: the origins of Ukraine's democratic breakthrough*. Washington D.C.: Carnegie Endowment for International Peace.

BBC. 2012. *Czechs stage huge anti-government rally in Prague*. BBC, April 21.

Beissinger, M.R., 2002. *Nationalist mobilization and the collapse of the Soviet State*. Cambridge: Cambridge University Press.

Bierschenk, Thomas (2018). In Chardu Sudan Kasturi *When Tiny Benin Shook Dictatores Across Africa*. https://www.ozy.com/flashback/when-tiny-benin-shook-dictators-across-africa/84008 Accessed 2019-05-30

Bonner, R., 1987. *Waltzing with a dictator: the Marcoses and the making of American policy*. New York: Times Books.

Bratton, M. & Van De Walle, N., 1992. Popular Protest and Political Reform in Africa. *Comparative Politics*, 24, 419-442.

Bratton, M. & Van De Walle, N., 1997. *Democratic experiments in Africa: regime transitions in comparative perspective*. NY, Cambridge University Press.

Bunce, V. & Wolchik, S.L., 2011. *Defeating authoritarian leaders in postcommunist countries*. Cambridge: Cambridge University Press.

Chenoweth, E. and M. J. Stephan (2011). *Why civil resistance works: the strategic logic of nonviolent conflict*. New York, Columbia University Press.

Cirtautas, A.M., 1997. *The Polish solidarity movement: revolution, democracy and natural rights*. London: Routledge.

Claffey, P., 2007. Kérékou the Chamelon, Master of Myth. In J.C. Strauss & D.C. O'Brian (eds.) *Staging Politics: Power and Performance in Asia and Africa*. London: I. B. Tauris, 91-110.

Clark, J.F. & Gardinier, D.E., 1997. *Political reform in Francophone Africa*. Boulder: Westview Press.

Cohan, A.S., 1975. *Theories of revolution: an introduction.* New York: Wiley.

Collin, M., 2007. *The time of the rebels : youth resistance movements and 21st century revolutions.* London: Serpent's Tail.

Collins, R.O. & Burns, J.M., 2007. *A history of Sub-Saharan Africa.* Cambridge: Cambridge University Press.

Decalo, S., 1997. Benin: First of the New Democracies. In J.F. Clark & D.E. Gardinier (eds.) *Political reform in Francophone Africa.* Boulder: Westview Press, 43-61.

Dunkerley, J., 1984. *Rebellion in the veins: political struggle in Bolivia, 1952-82.* London: Verso.

Foran, J., 1994. *A century of revolution: social movements in Iran.* Minneapolis: University of Minnesota Press.

Forssman, B., 2009. *Latvia's Penguin Revolution.* Euro-Topics.

Ganji, M., 2002. *Defying the Iranian revolution: from a minister to the Shah to a leader of resistance.* Westport: Praeger.

Gardner, L.C., 2011. *The road to Tahrir Square : Egypt and the United States from the rise of Nasser to the fall of Mubarak.* New York: New Press.

Gbado, B., 1990. *En Marche vers liberté: préludes du renouveau démocrattique au Bénin, un document historique, crise de 1989 au Bénin.* Contonou: T. Syndicat National Des Enseignements Secondaire, Et Professionel.

Gisselquist, R.M., 2008. Democratic Transition and Democratic Survival in Benin. *Democratization,* 15, 789-814.

Goodwin, J., 1994. Toward a New Sociology of Revolutions. *Theory and Society,* 23, 731-766.

Grix, J., 2000. *The role of the masses in the collapse of the GDR.* Houndmills: Macmillan Press.

Gurr, T.R., 1970. *Why men rebel.* Princeton: Princeton University Press.

Gutiérrez, G., 1973. *A theology of liberation: history, politics, and salvation*. Maryknoll: Orbis Books.

Harbeson, J.W., Rothchild, D.S. & Chazan, N., 1994. *Civil society and the state in Africa*. Boulder: L. Rienner Publishers.

Heilbrunn, J.R., 1993. Social Origins of National Conferences in Benin and Togo. *Journal of Modern African Studies*, 31, 277-299.

Heilbrunn, J.R., 1997. Commerce, Politics, and Business Associations in Benin and Togo. *Comparative Politics*, 29, 473-492.

Heldmann, M., 2013. *Ethnic Groups in Benin*. IMPETUS Atlas Benin. Köln: IMPETUS.

Hiller, H.H., 1983. Humor And Hostility: A Neglected Aspect Of Social Movement Analysis. *Qualitative Sociology*, 6, 255.

Hooglund, E.J., 1982. *Land and revolution in Iran, 1960-1980*. Austin: University of Texas Press.

Houngnikpo, M.C., *Determinants of Democratization in Africa, A Comparative Study of Benin and Togo*, University Press of America

Houtart, F. & Rousseau, A., 1971. *The church and revolution; from the French Revolution of 1789 to the Paris riots of 1968, from Cuba to Southern Africa, from Vietnam to Latin America*. Maryknoll: Orbis Books.

Huffington Post. 2009. Latvia's government resigns amid economic crisis. *Huffington Post*.

IRIN. 2005. BENIN: Kerekou says will retire next year, will not change constitution to stay in power. *IRIN Humanitarian News and Analysis*, July 12.

Johansen, J., 2009. External financing of oppositional Movements. In H. Clark (ed.) *People Power, Unarmed Resistance and Global Solidarity*. New York: Pluto Press, 198-205.

Johansen, J., 2010. Analysing External Support to Nonviolent Revolutions. In J. Johansen & J.Y. Jones (eds.) *Experiments with Peace, Celebrating Peace on Johan Galtung's 80th Birthday*. Oxford: Pambazuka Press, 103-114.

Kandiâc, N. & Fond Za Humanitarno Pravo., 2001. *Police crackdown on Otpor.* Belgrade: Humanitarian Law Center.

Karumize, Z. & Wertsch, J.V., 2005. *Enough!: the Rose Revolution in the Republic of Georgia, 2003.* New York: Nova Science Publishers.

Kneib, M., 2006. *Benin.* Tarrytown, N.Y.: Marshall Cavendish Benchmark.

Knudsen, A.J. & Kerr, M., 2012. *Lebanon: after the Cedar Revolution.* London: Hurst.

Korany, B. & El-Mahdi, R., 2012. *Arab spring in Egypt: revolution and beyond.* New York: The American University in Cairo Press.

Krushnelnycky, A., 2006. *An orange revolution: a personal journey through Ukrainian history.* London: Secker & Warburg.

Kulish, N., 2009. Hungary's Premier Offers to Resign. *The New York Times,* March 21.

Kuzio, T., 2005. From Kuchma to Yushchenko: Ukraine's 2004 Presidential Elections and the Orange Revolution. *Problems of Post-Communism,* 52, 29-44.

Kuzio, T. & Wilson, A., 1994. *Ukraine: Perestroika to independence.* New York: St. Martin's Press.

Laloupo, F., 1993. La conférence nationale du Bénin: Un concept nouveau de changement de régime politique. *Année Africaine,* 89-114.

Legters, L.H., 1992. *Eastern Europe: transformation and revolution, 1945-1991: documents and analyses.* Lexington: D.C. Heath.

Luxmoore, J. & Babiuch, J., 1999. *The Vatican and the red flag: the struggle for the soul of Eastern Europe.* London: G. Chapman.

Makumbe, J., 1998. Is there a civil society in Africa? *International Affairs,* 74, 305-317.

Malloy, J.M. & Gamarra, E., 1988. *Revolution and reaction: Bolivia, 1964-1985.* New Brunswick: Transaction Books.

Martin, B., 2007. *Justice ignited: the dynamics of backfire.* Lanham: Rowman & Littlefield Pub.

McAdam, D., et al. (2001). *Dynamics of contention*. Cambridge ; New York, Cambridge University Press.

Monga, C., 1995. Civil Society and Democratisation in Francophone Africa. *Journal of Modern African Studies*, Vol 33, Issue 3, pp. 359-379.

Mu, Y., Thompson, M.V. & China Dissident Collection (Library of Congress), 1989. *Crisis at Tiananmen: reform and reality in modern China*. San Francisco: China Books & Periodicals.

Nayar, S., 1989. *Mahatma Gandhi Vol IV, Satyagraha at Work*. Ahmedabad: Navajivan Publishing House.

Nepstad, S. E. (2011). *Nonviolent revolutions: civil resistance in the late 20th century*. Oxford, Oxford University Press.

Nkinyangi, J.A., 1991. Student Protests in Sub-Saharan Africa. *Higher Education*, 22, 157-173.

Noueihed, L. & Warren, A., 2012. *The battle for the Arab Spring: revolution, counter-revolution and the making of a new era*. New Haven: Yale University Press.

Nugent, P., 2004. *Africa since independence: a comparative history*. New York: Palgrave Macmillan.

Nwajiaku, K., 1994. The National Conferences in Benin and Togo Revisited. *Journal of Modern African Studies*, 32, 429-447.

Nzouankeu, J.M., 1993. The Role of the National Conference in the Transition to Democracy in Africa: The Cases of Benin and Mali. *A Journal of Opinion*, 21, 44-50.

Opp, K.-D., Voss, P. & Gern, C., 1995. *Origins of a spontaneous revolution: East Germany 1989*. Ann Arbor: University of Michigan Press.

Paulson, J., 2005. Removing the Dictator in Serbia - 1996-2000. In G. Sharp (ed.) *Waging Nonviolent Struggle: 20th Century Practice and 21st Century Potential*. Boston: Extending Horizons Books, 315-340.

Peczak, M. & Krajewska-Wieczorek, A., 1991. The Orange Ones, the Street, and the Background. *Performing Arts Journal*, 13, 50-55.

Peralta, A., 1990. ...*med andra medel: från Clausewitz till Guevara : krig, revolution och politik i en marxistisk idétradition* [...by other means : from Clausewitz to Guevara : war, revolution and politics in the Marxist tradition of ideas], Göteborg: Daidalos.

Petersen, R.D., 2001. *Resistance and rebellion: lessons from Eastern Europe*. New York: Cambridge University Press.

Phelan, C. (2011). "West African Trade Unionism Past and Present", p. 1-22, in C. Phelan (ed.) *Trade Unions in West Africa: Historical and Contemporary Perspectives*, Vol. 7, Peter Lang AG: Bern.

Pyarelal, 1980. *Mahama Gandhi Vol II, The Discovery of Satyagraha - On the Threshold*. Ahmedabad: Navajivan Publishing House.

Pyarelal, 1986. *Mahatma Gandhi Vol III, The Birth of Satyagraha*. Ahmedabad: Navajivan Publishing House.

Ranger, T.O., 1986. Religious Movements and Politics in Sub-Saharan Africa. *African Studies Review*, 29, 1-69.

Reuters. 2009. Iceland protesters demand government step down *Reuters*, Januray 20.

Reuters. 2013. Bulgarian government resigns amid protests over high electricity costs. *The Guardian*, February 20.

Ritter, D., 2013. Inside the Iron Cage of Liberalism: International Contexts and Nonviolent Success in the Iranian Revolution. In S. E. Nepstad & S. R. Kurtz (eds.) *Nonviolent Conflict and Civil Resistance*. Emerald Group Publishing Ltd., 95-121.

Roberts, A. and T. Garton Ash (2009). *Civil resistance and power politics: the experience of non-violent action from Gandhi to the present*. Oxford, Oxford University Press.

Salisbury, H.E., 1989. *Tiananmen diary: thirteen days in June*. Boston: Little Brown.

Sarotte, M.E., 2009. *1989: the struggle to create post-Cold War Europe*. Princeton, N.J.: Princeton University Press.

Schirmer, D.B. & Shalom, S.R., 1987. *The Philippines reader: a history of colonialism, neocolonialism, dictatorship, and resistance.* Boston: South End Press.

Schock, K. (2005). *Unarmed insurrections : people power movements in nondemocracies.* Minneapolis, University of Minnesota Press.

Scott, J.C., 1985. *Weapons of the weak: everyday forms of peasant resistance.* New Haven: Yale University Press.

Scott, J.C., 1990. *Domination and the arts of resistance: hidden transcripts.* New Haven: Yale University Press.

Sebestyen, V., 2010. *Revolution 1989: the fall of the Soviet empire.* New York: Pantheon Books.

Seely, J.C., 2001. *Transition to Democracy in Comparative Perspective: The National Conferences in Benin and Togo.* Washington University.

Seely, J.C., 2005. The legacies of transition governments: post-transition dynamics in Benin and Togo. *Democratization,* 12, 357-377.

Seely, J.C., 2009. *The legacies of transition governments in Africa: the cases of Benin and Togo.* New York: Palgrave Macmillan.

Sixsmith, M., 1991. *Moscow coup: the death of the Soviet system.* New York: Simon & Schuster.

Skocpol, T., 1979. *States and social revolutions : a comparative analysis of France, Russia, and China.* New York: Cambridge University Press.

Stjernø, S., 2005. *Solidarity in Europe: the history of an idea.* Cambridge: Cambridge University Press.

Tilly, C., 2004. *Social movements, 1768-2004.* Boulder: Paradigm Publishers.

U.S. State Department, 2007. *Benin.* Washington: U.S.S. Department.

Unicef, 2013. *Statistics for Benin* [online]. UNICEF. Available from: http://www.unicef.org/infobycountry/benin_statistics.html [Accessed February 6 2013].

Unites Nations Population Fund, 2011. *The State of the World's Midwifery.* New York.

Vinthagen, S., 2005. *Ickevåldsaktion : en social praktik av motstånd och konstruktion* [Nonviolent Action : A Social Practice of Resistance and Construction] Göteborg: Institutionen för freds- och utvecklingsforskning (PADRIGU) Göteborgs universitet.

Waterfield, B. 2009. Protesters pelt car of Icelandic prime minister. *The Telegraph*, January 21.

Wheaton, B. & Kavan, Z., 1992. *The Velvet Revolution: Czechoslovakia, 1988-1991.* Boulder: Westview Press.

Widner, J.A., 1994. *Economic change and political liberalization in Sub-Saharan Africa.* Baltimore: Johns Hopkins University Press.

Wilson, A., 2005. *Ukraine's Orange Revolution.* New Haven: Yale University Press.

Yu, M.C. & Harrison, J.F., 1990. *Voices from Tiananmen Square: Beijing Spring and the democracy movement.* Montréal: New York: Black Rose Books.

Zajovic, S. & Aleksov, B., 1997. *Women for peace Beograd: Women in black.*

Zolberg, A.R., 1968. The Structure of Political Conflict in the New States of Tropical Africa. *The American Political Science Review,* 62, 70-87.

Available also as e-book

This important book by a famous Thai Muslim--theoretician and practitioner-- carries a double message. First, it puts to shame those who equate Islam with violence and terrorism, often called "jihadism" in a total misunderstanding of jihad. Second. it also puts to shame those who classify entire religions as violent or nonviolent; they may have both aspects, let us identify and build on the nonviolence, and move forward!

Johan Galtung, Founder Transcend International, Dr hc mult

Available also as e-book with fantastic graphic illustrations

Ever wondered what it's like to feel so strongly about an issue that you'll go to jail for it? This novel, based on real-life environmental blockades but set within a humorous sci-fi universe, is a journey to the centre of nonviolent civil disobedience by an author who has been there repeatedly over decades. In a hilarious romp through the universe we meet eco-pirates, space heroines, Indigenous people and farmers united against corporate greed, corrupt governments and environmental destruction.

www.irenepublishing.com

The leading international academic journal on resistance:

JOURNAL OF RESISTANCE STUDIES

JRS is an international, interdisciplinary and peer-reviewed scientific journal that explores unarmed resistance. The focus is on critical understandings of resistance strategies, discourses, tactics, effects, causes, contexts and experiences. Our aim is to advance an understanding of how resistance might undermine repression, injustices and domination of any kind, as well as how resistance might nurture autonomous subjectivity, as e.g. constructive work, alternative communities, oppositional ways of thinking. We invite journal articles or book reviews and debate contributions.

SUBSCRIPTIONS

Through our website www.resistance-journal.org you can order single articles or subscribe and get immediate access to all open access issues and articles. We make all articles and issues open access two years after publication.

You will need a credit card to make a payment online. To pay by check, please contact orders@resistance-journal.org. Checks need to be made out to: University of Massachusetts Amherst Resistance Studies Journal.

Institution can also go through:
EBSCO: **https://journals.ebsco.com**

or

WT.Cox: **http://www.wtcox.com**

www.ingramcontent.com/pod-product-compliance
Lightning Source LLC
LaVergne TN
LVHW021625080426
835510LV00019B/2759